W9-CRW-301

A
CORPORATE BESTIARY

Or, How to

Spot the Animals

in Your Organization

by William G. Zikmund

with illustrations by Nancy Blackwood

An Owl Book • HOLT, RINEHART AND WINSTON • NEW YORK

Published in January 1986 by Holt, Rinehart
and Winston, 383 Madison Avenue, New York,
New York 10017. Published simultaneously in Canada
by Holt, Rinehart and Winston of Canada, Limited.

Library of Congress Cataloging in Publication Data
Zikmund, William G.
A corporate bestiary, or, How to spot the animals
in your organization.
"An Owl book."
1. Business—Anecdotes, facetiae, satire, etc.
I. Blackwood, Nancy. II. Title. III. Title: Corporate
bestiary. IV. Title: How to spot the animals in your
organization.
PN6231.B85Z5 1986   650'.0207   85-22000
ISBN 0-03-002998-8 (pbk.)

First Edition

Designer: Madalyn Hart
Printed in the United States of America
10 9 8 7 6 5 4 3 2 1

ISBN 0-03-002998-8

CONTENTS

Preface   1

The Prestigious M.B.A.   2

The Inevitable Burnout   4

The Vanishing Secretary   6

Perks (A.K.A. Perquisites)   8

The Yea-Saying Fence-Sitter   10

The Hidden Agenda   12

The Workhorse   14

The Conventioneer   16

The Punctual Commuter   18

The Monday Morning   20

The Simple Answer   22

The Promotion and the Raise   24

The Mediocre Employee   26

The Word Processor   28

The Razzmatazz and the Pizzazz   30

Profits   32

The Short Sell   34

The Job Hopper   36

The Ubiquitous Committee   38

The Computer Analyst   40

The Second Shift   42

The Obfuscating Bureaucrat   44

The Up-and-Comer   46

The Venture Capitalist/
The Entrepreneurial Spirit   48

The Past Orientation   50

The Forecast   52

The Reorganization   54

The Good-Ole-Boy Network   56

The Power Struggle   58

The Recession   60

The Performance Appraisal   62

The Three-Piece Suit   64

The Potential Bankruptcy   66

Rules and Regulations   68

The Client   70

Facts   72

Jobs   74

The Strike   76

The Aggressive Sales Force   78

The U.S. Economy   80

The Economists   82

The Cash Cow   84

The Thirty-Second Commercial   86

The Carefree Vacation   88

The Golden Opportunity   90

Finis   92

PREFACE

A bestiary is a book of mythical as well as not-so-mythical beasts. In medieval times the bestiary served as a kind of field guide that described intriguing and possibly dangerous creatures—some imaginary, like the unicorn or phoenix, others, like the rhinoceros or giraffe, quite real but unbelievable—that lurked in dark forests and uncharted lands. When knights-errant roamed abroad to rescue damsels in distress and otherwise prove their prowess, they always consulted their bestiaries before venturing very far afield. Indeed, all travelers found that the wisdom of the bestiary helped prepare them to deal with dragons and other unpleasant situations.

Although modern adventurers no longer need worry about encountering a basilisk, the challenge of the unknown remains. In today's business world, the beasts have become less immediately recognizable, more subtle, and ever so much more cunning.

A Corporate Bestiary is a menagerie of whimsical but not always beguiling creatures that inhabit the organizational jungle. Some of these beasts are endangered species, while a few are possibly extinct, but many are known to proliferate with abandon. There are difficult-to-spot nocturnal animals, like the Hidden Agenda, although certain others—the Razzmatazz and the Pizzazz, for example—are all too conspicuous for their colorful and even flamboyant behavior.

It is important for the wayfarer to know which corporate beasts are playful and friendly and which are unpredictable and dangerous. Those latter-day knights who test their mettle against the perils of the corporate wilderness will find this bestiary an aid to survival. Its purpose is to help provide the best protection available in the business world: *a good sense of humor.*

1

THE PRESTIGIOUS M.B.A.

This quite highly pedigreed animal is not geographically dispersed evenly throughout the entire United States. It tends to be concentrated on the East Coast and in the San Francisco Bay area, though in recent years the area around the tip of Lake Michigan has shown evidence of this species.

Scientific classification of the M.B.A. is complex. For example, there are U.C.L.A. M.B.A.s and B.Y.U. M.B.A.s, as well as Northwestern M.B.A.s. The Cal State-Fullerton M.B.A. is not really a Prestigious M.B.A., but the Stanford M.B.A. is definitely the right kind.

Considered in evolutionary perspective, the M.B.A. is said to be the forerunner of the Promotion. In its final evolutionary stage, the Prestigious M.B.A. expands the potential span of the corporate life.

When domesticated, the M.B.A. tends to be shown off. The Harvard M.B.A. has won the most prizes, while the Executive M.B.A., although more expensive than other M.B.A.s, is recognized to be an inferior breed.

Organizational members without the M.B.A frequently comment that inbreeding and experience are more important. They believe M.B.A.s are full of B.S.

THE INEVITABLE BURNOUT

The Burnout, a direct descendant of Depression and a close relative of the Nervous Breakdown, is found everywhere from the boardroom to the air traffic controller's tower. This frustrated, middle-aged beast is past its prime and no longer has an appetite for accomplishments. The Burnout has been at it too many years, put up with too much nonsense, and no longer gets involved. Without drive or determination, it merely puts in its time waiting for five P.M. The Burnout wears an invisible sign saying "out of business." If you sit in the executive suite long enough, the Burnout will inevitably appear.

THE VANISHING SECRETARY

This is an endangered species. The dictating machine, word-processing equipment, and the Women's Liberation Movement have hastened its destruction. The entire disgruntled breed may soon be wiped out. Finding the typing, personal shopping, coffee making, "righthand man" Secretary today is almost impossible. It was once a purely female breed, hence the speculation by some that its long-term reproduction of progeny was doomed from the start. Others argue that its pursuit of more attractive Career Interests caused the Secretarial shortage.

PERKS (A.K.A. PERQUISITES)

It is not much fun to be in a company without Perks, which are very cheerful. Perks live lavishly and blissfully on the fringe of the corporate jungle. They display, even flaunt, their bright colors to others. Perks are the most enjoyable benefits of the executive suite. You may have to negotiate to get a Perk, but once you do, you know you have something extra.

Perks perform many useful tasks: free legal counseling, financial planning, education for offspring, even getting you to work each day. Without Perks, you might even have to ride a bus. After all, some Perks, like the Corvette and Cadillac, which are the favorite of this variety, have wheels. (It's better if Perks are made in America.)

The Expense Account is a large and especially colorful subspecies of the Perk family. This wonderful migratory creature travels south in the winter. It feeds, even indulges, without a worry of where its next meal is coming from. It appears fat to some, but appearance may be misleading, for it is often padded. The worst thing that can happen to the Expense Account is to have its wings clipped. To find one of these prize specimens look only in the best of places.

Perk activity is followed closely by the I.R.S. and the Audubon Society. Since Perks offer an alternative to Taxes, people wonder what Perks are worth. But who cares? After all, having or not having Perks is what really counts.

THE YEA-SAYING FENCE-SITTER

The Yea-Saying Fence-Sitter is very light in weight. Students of the bird explain this by suggesting they have no guts. Their small claws do not allow them to grasp issues well. As a result, they tend to go whichever way the wind blows.

This bird is a favorite of the autocratic manager because it is so palatable.

THE HIDDEN AGENDA

Unknown to many other beasts, the Hidden Agenda is rarely noticed. A favorite pet of ruthless administrators, the Hidden Agenda makes no ostentatious show of power. The Hidden Agenda merely creeps along with the Scheduled Agenda. A Hidden Agenda poses a very dangerous problem for those unaware of its existence: Although its appearance is similar to the False Pretense, the Hidden Agenda, with its Machiavellian nature, should not be confused with this honest creature. They are very different beasts.

THE WORKHORSE

The Workhorse, trained to work harder not smarter, comes in early and leaves late. The Workhorse has a very short nose because it keeps it to the grindstone for long periods of time. It frantically goes through the same motions over and over without any thought. Concentrating on input rather than output, it wonders why it never goes anywhere. Comparing its heart to its brain is like comparing a watermelon to a pea.

THE CONVENTIONEER

Veterinary psychiatrists say this animal is schizophrenic. It has one personality on its domestic turf and a totally different personality when it inhabits a foreign turf. The Conventioneer frequently travels to the wilderness of California. It may also be found in the Big Apple, the French Quarter, and at various other watering holes. During its annual migration, the beast dramatically changes its eating and drinking habits. Alcohol is consumed at all hours of the day and night. The beast begins to crave snails, abalone, and oysters. It may even consume raw fish. Sleeping patterns are radically adjusted.

A certain variety of Conventioneer changes its sexual behavior. This species, while normally monogamous, becomes quite promiscuous when aroused by the sight of the Hooker. Fortunately all changes in behavior, with the exception of the shrinking of the wallet muscle, are temporary. (Wallet problems may not occur if the Conventioneer travels with a company Expense Account.)

Conventioneers, with their loud boisterous talk and staggering strut, are very noticeable. Tags that say "Hi, I'm Skip" are a sure giveaway. The Shriner is the most colorful, easily identified by its long tassels on a purple crown. If there is still uncertainty, look for AKADAR-Toledo; a sure sign that one has spotted this wandering beast.

THE PUNCTUAL COMMUTER

The Punctual Commuter arrives at 8:22 and leaves at 5:17. It lives in Connecticut or Long Island but spends most of its time in New York City. There is a brief two-week period when it goes to Florida or the Caribbean or Cape Cod to get away from it all, albeit it then uses a different form of transportation.

The well-trained Punctual Commuter can be counted on, with considerable regularity, to follow the crowd. The sound of a whistle blowing elicits a reaction calling forth certain standardized behavior in transit. Commuters from Connecticut prefer the FILO method—First-In-Last-Off—whereas those from Jamaica Station utilize the FIFO method—First-in-First-Off—hoping to win the race out of the gate.

There have been reports of a rare Commuter who confuses altitude for latitude and longitude. Residing in Chicago on the seventy-first floor of the John Hancock tower, it commutes down and up rather than round and round on its way to work on twenty-two.

THE MONDAY MORNING

Every seventh day at the crack of dawn a Monday
Morning appears at organizations throughout America.
While it is similar in temperature and appearance to a
Friday Afternoon, the subtle differences are astounding.
You probably have heard someone thank goodness that
a Friday Afternoon has arrived, but such a welcome is
rarely expressed for Monday Morning even though
Monday Morning tries to be bright eyed and bushy
tailed. It is despised by many people, perhaps because it
is so predictable.

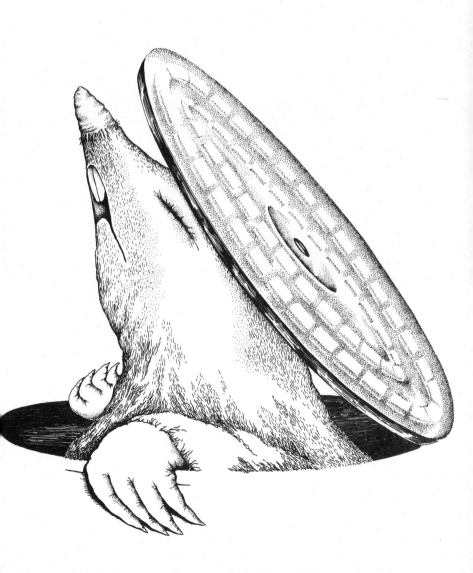

THE SIMPLE ANSWER

Some say this very rare and elusive breed no longer exists. And yet, searches for a Simple Answer still do frequently occur. An enormous amount of time is spent and reams of data are combed over looking for the Simple Answer. Paradoxically, these expeditions often are very complex.

Conditional Answers, surrounded by Ifs, Wherefores, and Buts, are much more abundant. Perhaps the evolutionary process has had its impact.

THE PROMOTION AND THE RAISE

This is truly a symbiotic relationship. The Promotion and the Raise often depend on each other. However, although the slow, lumbering Promotion is almost always accompanied by a Raise, Raises are seen frequently without Promotions.

The elusive Promotion can be quite formidable. Being hard to catch, they make good trophies. The resentful Promotion often feeds on rival species and intruders. Although barely visible, wounds on the Promotion's body are indicators of the terrific battles that may take place. Upon snaring the Promotion, the corporate hunter may display solicitude toward others in a similar situation.

The Raise is among the most popular creatures in the corporate bestiary. With the exception of a few in political office (where Hidden Agendas are prevalent), the Raise is rarely turned away. In fact, people often ask for them, but it is much better when they come your way unexpectedly.

THE MEDIOCRE EMPLOYEE

Although this beast has no special skills, it seems to outlive all other creatures. The reason for its amazing longevity is simple. It takes no chances. It never ventures into the unknown. It never triumphs. It never loses.

Observers, who have spent years existing with the beast in its natural habitat, suspect that the apparently mute Mediocre Employee actually does communicate with other beasts. The following utterances have been recorded on tape: "Not my job," "Not my department," and "Is it breaktime yet?" These data lead to the hypothesis, yet unproven, that Mediocre Employees may have an intelligence level equal to the lower primates.

THE WORD PROCESSOR

Part typewriter and part computer, the Word Processor is feared by those not of the computer age. It sits on desks hardly moving at all, relying on speed as its only defense against detractors. This amazingly versatile creature devours words, sentences, and paragraphs and regurgitates them as reports and memos. Many scholars find it impossible to believe the legend that the Word Processor's ancestor was the Pencil.

THE RAZZMATAZZ AND THE PIZZAZZ

Like peacocks, these birds are very colorful. Unlike peacocks, they have no claim to natural beauty. It has been said that at birth they are thrown up in the air, and if they fly, feathers are put on them. They are raised in advertising agencies, fed on words. This diet nourishes them so that they come in a variety of colors, in different sizes, and many unique patterns. Yet all have a recognizable bashful expression. Their images are stronger than their substances, which at times may be downright puny. The Razzmatazz and the Pizzazz have an uncanny ability to puff themselves up. When they do this, they are very seductive.

They prefer nesting among Madison Avenue's bright lights. However, occasionally they may be seen traveling door-to-door with the Demonstration, a bird that does well with a little Pizzazz.

PROFITS

Profits are found below the line. In fact, they are the bottom line. Do not confuse these with prophets who forecast the future. Of course Pro Forma Profits cloud this issue. In any case, Profits are carefully observed, especially by financial analysts. Everyone knows where they have been, but no one knows where they are going.

Always commanding attention, they may be the king of the corporate beasts. During growth spurts, they are pampered. Bigger and better Profits are idolized, but analysts are fickle. In Profits' declining years, they take on a foul odor, and Declining Profits, usually found in the same areas as Market Share Reductions and Cost Overruns, are barely tolerable.

THE SHORT SELL

The Short Sell is difficult to understand. Most of its aggressive movements are the reverse of what is considered normal. With its keen sense of anticipation, its motto is "Look Ahead." Speed serves as its defense against its enemies. Constantly darting in and out of hedges provides its bread and butter, coconut oil, wheat, and alfalfa. Of course, it also craves pork bellies (whatever they are). A thick skin is necessary for survival of the Short Sell as it must have the ability to bounce back. Sells consider an enemy to be any beast that forces it to deliver truckloads of soybeans to Decatur, Illinois.

THE JOB HOPPER

Job Hoppers are not loyal to the territory. Whenever greener grass is imagined elsewhere, the Hopper definitely moves to the new pasture. Since they are always going from place to place, their resumes are greatly enlarged. A Hopper that displays its resume is signaling that it is ready for a new mate. This promiscuous species does not exist in Japan, where one's own corporate pasture is always greener. In Japan, everyone lives and works in the same pasture, never venturing beyond it.

Like the locust, the Job Hopper periodically becomes more numerous. During times of economic prosperity, jumping from one job to another increases exponentially. This ceaseless multiplying abruptly stops in the face of Recessions.

Job Hoppers should not be confused with Job Hunters. Often unskilled and untrained, Job Hunters are far less desirable. Many, unless they are the CETA variety, do not own alarm clocks. Job Hunters find themselves in the worst kind of predicament. In the jungle the paradoxical logic is that those best qualified for a job do not need a job. Thus, if it is known you really need it, you won't get it.

THE UBIQUITOUS COMMITTEE

The Committee is everywhere. This ungainly group of animals is careful never to stick out its collective neck. Individual beasts are rarely seen as they carefully hide themselves among the others. The pattern of no responsibility decision making, a distinguishing feature, is strikingly displayed on the hide of the Committee. It serves as a perfect camouflage, rendering the individuals within the Committee almost invisible. Even close inspection of the Committee does not allow for identifying individual responsibility.

It is well known that a zebra is a horse designed by a Committee. A lesser known fact is that Committees are capable of asexual reproduction by breaking off a part of the parent animal. The offspring are known as *Ad Hoc* Committees whose sole purpose is to postpone decisions.

The hindsight of the Ubiquitous Committee is wonderful, on the other hand its foresight is extremely poor. A unique feature of the Committee, the complete absence of insight, surprises corporate neophytes. Older, more worldly observers are rarely surprised by anything a Committee does.

Although the Committee was known to the ancient Egyptians and was featured in the Roman senate, its proper place within the corporation has only comparatively recently been understood. This has been made possible not only by the strides of scientists studying organizational behavior, but by the discovery that most Committee decisions are grossly wrong.

THE COMPUTER ANALYST

Outsiders call the Computer Analyst a freak. A human mutation, Computer Analysts speak in binary, hexadecimal, and other strange tongues. Very systematic, especially about interactive systems, application systems, software systems, and general systems, Computer Analysts don't think like the rest of us. Computer Analysts have delusions about a general system to portray the grand scheme of all things. Shunned by others, the way of the Computer Analyst is to abstract human interaction as an irrelevant variable. People don't matter in the Computer Analyst's system. These little big men who see themselves as in control may be trapped easily: Go to the program, follow the looping pattern, and ask an "If/Then" question.

THE SECOND SHIFT

Different is the best word to describe the Second Shift.
It spends most of its time in the dark. This nocturnal
creature eats at strange times, confuses Sunday for
Monday, and does not associate with other corporate beasts, especially those with white collars or
seniority. A shift differential is required to keep it happy
at feeding time.

THE OBFUSCATING BUREAUCRAT

The Obfuscating Bureaucrat wallows in mud and prefers murky water for its buck-passing ritual. This instinctual behavior, performed so that the public and press are unaware of the true nature of the Bureaucrat's actions, assures one that a manager is not confused for a Bureaucrat. Bureaucrats spend most of their day reporting on what they are doing, rather than doing anything. Its mumbled verbiage (also called gobbledygook) is difficult to decipher. However, after years of difficult study, scholars now agree that communication among Bureaucrats is altogether impossible.

The Bureaucrat's migration pattern is toward the dead-end job, and there is no need for Bureaucrats to hurry. Some naturalists argue that the Bureaucrat's speed, or lack of it, is the predominant cause of its enormous size. Since this argument is consistent with the view that its bulk has grown much faster than its brain, it is widely accepted.

Bureaucrats who thrive on apathy prefer not-for-profit organizations to profit-making organizations. The U.S. Postal Service, abundant with apathy, is a federally supported preserve for this species. Here relaxed Bureaucrats engage busily in exercising the Cost Overrun.

THE UP-AND-COMER

The Up-and-Comer scrambles on the fast track. Desperately and aggressively seeking the upper echelon, its only movement is upward. Climbing to the top is the be-all and the end-all of its existence. Anything goes. Fiercely competitive, it may devour its peers. In its quest for preeminence, the Up-and-Comer displays great ingenuity to hide its own weaknesses behind a Subordinate's talent. Survival is a finely honed skill. Attacking easy prey is the fastest way for the ruthless to get ahead. The Subordinate's relationship with the Up-and-Comer is very critical. Like the praying mantis who eats its mate after sex, the Up-and-Comer sends the unsuspecting Subordinate heading off to nowhere when it is no longer useful.

Arch rivals worry the Up-and-Comer because mirror reflections are difficult to defeat.

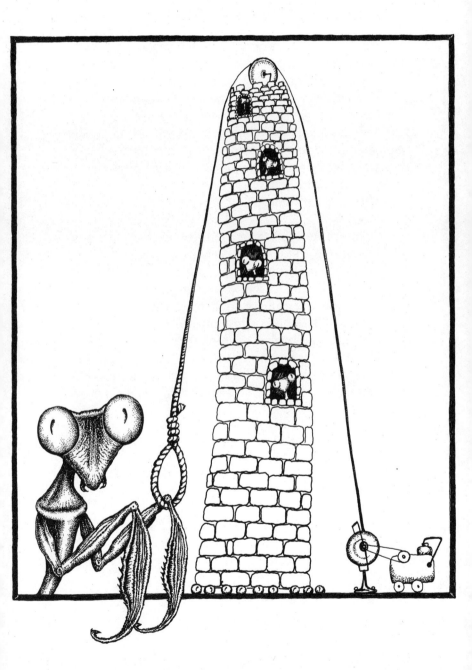

THE VENTURE CAPITALIST/
THE ENTREPRENEURIAL SPIRIT

Venture Capitalists are gamblers always seeking new
territory. In this risky business a portion of the pie can
amount to a fortune. Venture Capitalists who are natu-
rally fat, normally from inheritance, are instinctively
lured by optimism. They believe that following the
lucrative funding route of their parent is possible. Too
often, the son is not the equal of the father. But the
Sangfroid Venture Capitalist seems to have too many
inherited advantages to lose all. Indeed, it is said it is
able to endure fire and all other forms of heat before
perishing.

The Entrepreneurial Spirit requires the companionship
of the Venture Capitalists. The Venture Capitalist is wooed
by Entrepreneurial Spirits who make themselves as
attractive as possible. When young they feed on dreams,
which are uplifting, but not nourishing. They fantasize
that mating with Venture Capitalists will produce a
stronger enlarged offspring. Later, most learn this mating
dream is overly optimistic. If the union has been performed with too much leverage, the 1 to 100 long-shot
progeny never develops. Nonproductive offspring are 99
to 1 shots.

THE PAST ORIENTATION

The Past Orientation reflects on the successful years of past decades. For years, Past Orientations at companies like Robert Hall, A&P, and Korvettes managed to run their business without rocking the boat. On the surface, the sea appeared calm. Those who warned of a changing environment were told, "If it worked in the past, why shouldn't it work in the future? Don't argue with success!" With their heads in the sand, these animals point backward.

N. BLACKWOOD

THE FORECAST

Forecasts, like the swallows of Capistrano, reappear with predictable regularity. Forecasts, however, come in a much wider range of sizes and in many varieties. The Long-Range Forecast is quite different from the Short-Range Forecast, because the duration of the projected migratory flight is substantially greater. The Sales Forecast is generally the largest and most powerful of all the Forecasts and other Forecasts tend to follow its lead blindly. The Flexible Forecast adapts chameleon-like to the changing environment. It reacts, albeit slowly, to the behavior of such foes as Predatory Competitors and others who attempt to disturb The Forecast's pattern.

Training these unpredictable beasts is not accomplished without considerable difficulty. In captivity, Forecasts have been known to be unreliable and they often disagree with each other. Forecasts that do not fly are often blamed on unanticipated factors, even the weather. With a tendency toward irregularity, the disposition of Forecasts may be somewhat unpleasant. Few people ever like them; even among themselves there is disdain for the species. Many call Forecasts stupid.

Older Forecasts, bearing the scars of youth, tend to be cautiously optimistic. This optimism may be dampened if Forecasts are caught expanding in a down economy. It is at this time that Forecasts are most vulnerable.

THE REORGANIZATION

Observing the Reorganization from conception to maturity is fascinating. In some cases it is miraculous to see meager and almost useless parts grow in dramatic disproportion to other organs. Many bizarre mutations have occurred. For instance, single-headed Organizations have been abnormally transformed into three-headed divisional beasts. Developing Reorganizations may go through several transitional stages, each stage more awkward than the one that preceded it. One of the wonders of corporate life is that phoenixlike, Reorganizations may return to the same state they were in fifteen years earlier. The new Reorganization becomes the old Organization, everyone is placed back in the same job.

Consultants, who have spent a great deal of time investigating Organizations and Reorganizations, lack a single good theory for Organizational growth. The Reorganization is difficult to study, especially if it is accompanied by the Bloodbath or Shakeup. At these times, no one is safe. Even formal lines of authority may not control the awesome beast's behavior.

THE GOOD-OLE-BOY NETWORK

Did this species originate in Texas? There is no agree-
ment among Network scholars. Although they agree
unanimously this is a Southern Phenomenon, many argue
that these critters developed simultaneously in numerous
pockets of Dixie. Armadillo-like, the Good-Ole-Boy Network has a protective shell. It moves slowly along,
fiercely protecting its own kind. While this canny beast is
generally friendly, it has been known to be ugly, cruel,
and deplorably violent when provoked.

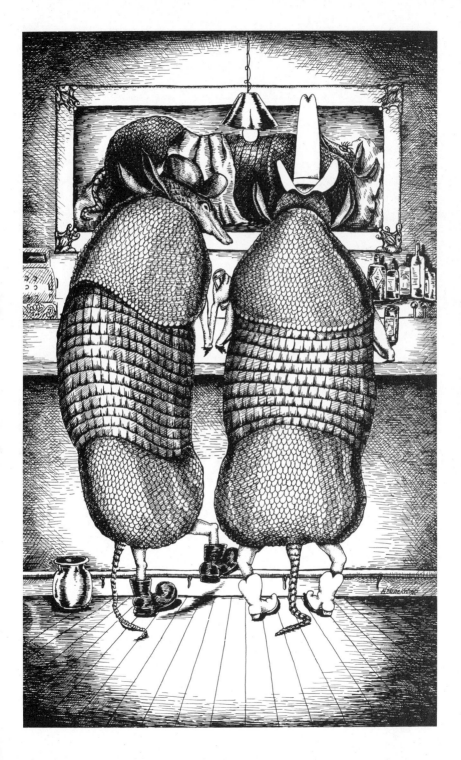

THE POWER STRUGGLE

The Bureaucratic Skirmish, which leaves an odor wherever it goes, is followed by the Power Struggle. Power Struggles are most populous during the mating season. The older, more seasoned males are usually the first to recognize the breeding grounds before the continual warfare is begun. The seasoned animals take care to identify the battle turf and maintain their particular piece of ground. The younger animals rarely recognize their plight until it is too late. They look beyond, seeing only the spoils and the trophy normally awarded the winner. Too often the young ones go it alone, only to find the seasoned veterans have many accomplices. Alas, locking horns in turf battles creates many casualties and most Struggles are short lived. One's day in the sun, although relished, does not last. Hence, timing is everything to the Power Struggle.

The Hidden Agenda may often be seen in the background, since it follows the same course as the Power Struggle.

THE RECESSION

The Recession, also called the Downturn, is an omnivore. Although it consumes everything, it prefers Profits. Workers run for security to avoid the Unemployment line when the Recession is in the jungle. According to legend, Unemployment is an evil spirit said to have been hatched from a Recession's egg. Unemployment haunts towns, driving people to faraway places like Tulsa and Houston.

Recessions may be blamed for things whether they caused them or not. Incompetents often blame the Recession for internal problems. The man who doesn't lock the chicken house door claims that it was the Recession who consumed the chickens. While they do not eat chickens, left uncontrolled for long periods Recessions can cause damage. Layoffs surge, Inventories dwindle, and Orders are cut back.

Hunters and Economists lately have been aiming at the supply side of the Recession. The pay cut is a popular managerial technique to eliminate fat from its carcass. On the other hand, the tax cut is an elixir expected to turn the Recession around. Strange, although the Recession is not sick everyone hopes to sight a Recovery on the horizon.

THE PERFORMANCE APPRAISAL

The Performance Appraisal is distinguished by its shrill wail, a sound something like "what-have-you-done-for-me-lately." This cry is made seasonally, not year round. It spends most of its time submerged, out-of-sight, but like the salmon, its basic function must be periodically performed. Watching and evaluating its prey without being noticed is basic to its nature. Sometimes this is difficult because the Performance Appraisal may be blind in one eye. It favors the Token Woman, but dislikes aged creatures. It aggressively attacks beasts over fifty years of age.

Its trainers, down in personnel, have told it to be equitable and to suppress its instinct for surprise attack. The Buck Passer must watch out for the Appraisal because the Appraisal is not always objective; it often does only what it wants.

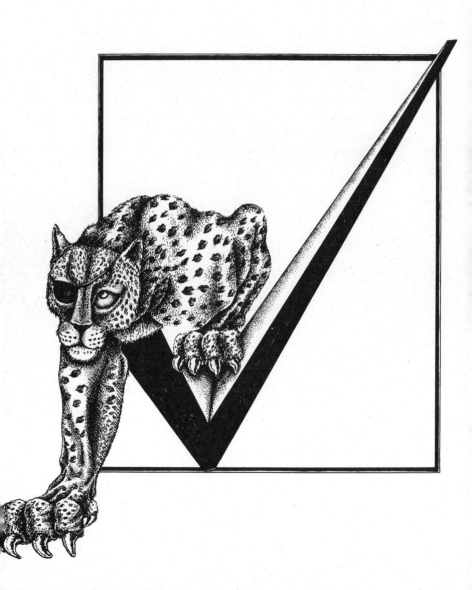

THE THREE-PIECE SUIT

The Three-Piece Suit is very common, but not necessarily uniform. Although at times other colors are seen, the majority are navy blue or gray. In Washington, D.C., the Three-Piece Suit has a pin-striped pattern, a variety never seen on the West Coast. At IBM, where they are quite somber and travel with White Button-Down Shirts, they are believed to have magical qualities. In fact, many people believe this creature has the power to create an illusion. Supposedly the Three-Piece Suit magically transforms a clod into an executive. However, insiders know that when you look at a Three-Piece Suit in a mirror all you can see is an image.

—

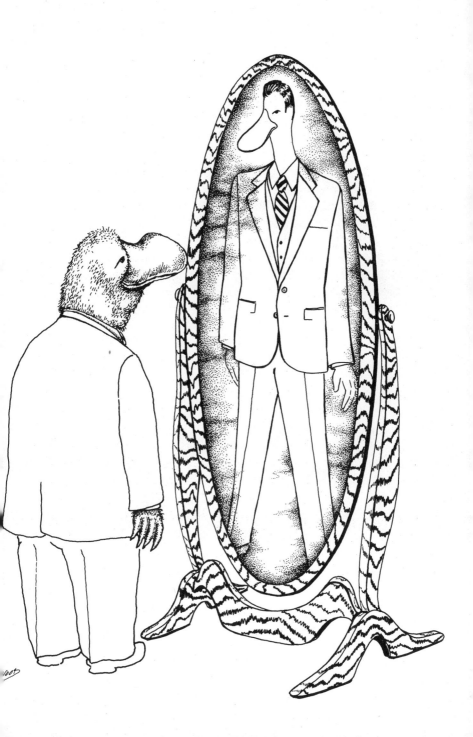

THE POTENTIAL BANKRUPTCY

Wall Street experts are always on the lookout for this troublesome creature. It is a constant threat to unwary investors. Reclusive, it usually hides in the forest behind a protective cover provided by accountants. Detection may be difficult, especially when managers can't see the forest for the trees.

The Potential Bankruptcy becomes more noticeable if it leaves the forest and begins to travel downhill. The Bankruptcy may be quite elusive until, all of a sudden, it encounters the Perilous Setback. Too many observers follow Setbacks. The Potential Bankruptcy loses its protective cover. At this point, the beast becomes dangerous. A cornered animal will do anything to survive. Mating with the most undesirable of partners, such as the Loathed Competitor, may occur. After meeting its first Setback, the ailing beast tries to avoid other encounters by inching toward a treacherous ally, the Financial Reorganization. If this tactic does work, the Bankruptcy may strike without warning. It may make an abrupt replacement. The ritualistic move is an attempt to soothe creditors by pretending it has the resurgent power of a phoenix. Pink Slips begin to circle like vultures.

Perhaps the most unusual characteristic of this creature is that it can read, but it never goes beyond chapter XI.

RULES AND REGULATIONS

These two beasts are identical. Nevertheless, they are given different names. That is the way bureaucrats do things. Rules and Regulations, having been domesticated for centuries, are found everywhere. Rules and Regulations, like cats, are either intensely loved or hated. The most interesting thing about them is how people react to them. There are two types of individuals in organizations: those who like to play *by* the Rules and those who like to play *with* the Rules. The former are unbending. Everything is, without deviation, by the book. Of course, the rulebook is always called something else. Employee handbook or divisional policy statement are common euphemisms.

Those who play with Rules and Regulations like to have their own way. They love the risk of breaking the Rules. "Productive" and "goal oriented" are words they use to describe themselves. Playing with the Rules may mean you take a stand or stick your neck out. Sitting back, playing it safe, and hoping for miracles is not the temperament of those who are playing with the Rules. Some people say that it is harder to break the Rules today.

Women have to play by men's Rules. But this does not appear in the employee handbook. There are Unwritten Rules. Some are more sacred than totems and taboos. For example it may be politically wise never to be responsible for killing an idea. Unwritten Rules must be followed.

THE CLIENT

Salesmen, lawyers, and advertising agencies are always trying to snare the Client. The abundant stories about this wily old game bird almost all begin by comparing it to the goose that lays golden eggs. Nesting on a great treasure, consisting of fees, commissions, and contracts, it has a universal attraction. Some say obtaining the cherished treasure is more trouble than it is worth because Clients are unreasonable. One allegory tells how it is possible to break your back trying to please the bewitching (or is it bitching?) Client.

Many ingenious traps have been used to entice Clients, but snaring the Client is not easy. It must be coddled, not hunted. Food is one of the more common lures. The Client feeds on an exotic diet, always whatever it wants, in the best of places. Throughout the Four Seasons, it eats and drinks. After a series of large meals and banquets, the Prospective Client is expected to part with its treasure. This may not occur. Always unpredictable, Clients may choose to hibernate or to eat the bait of another hunter. Then, at the oddest times, with the greatest sense of urgency, it charges aggressively toward its suitor. To achieve a union, the suitor may be forced into a compromising position, which makes the longed-for Client's treasure appear more like Eve's apple than a golden egg. But this may be better than sour grapes.

FACTS

Facts abound. Accountants, marketing researchers, and almost every manager has his pet Facts. Facts may be trained to do exactly what you want, which accounts for their popularity.

Facts may be very helpful or very harmful. Too often Facts are taken for granted at which time they are even more dangerous than Hidden Facts. It has been said that "It's not the things we don't know that get us in trouble, its the things we know that ain't so." So know your Facts.

JOBS

There are millions and millions of Jobs. While the Job population is expanding, there never seem to be enough. In some circles people who have Jobs are considered to be fortunate. Yet, many Jobs are dreary; some are dirty. Some people hate their Jobs; for them holding a Job requires too much work. To these people, Jobs are irritating, something that spoils the picnic.

Apparently, Jobs consume a great deal of oxygen. This must be so because people are always saying their Jobs don't give them enough breathing space. On the other hand, some people can hardly stand a weekend away from their Jobs. Their Jobs are described as exciting, interesting, and challenging. People from South of the Border find Jobs so popular (even the Demeaning Job) they will leave their families for them. The reasons for this dichotomy is one of the more controversial subjects in Jobology. Whether people like their Jobs or not, everyone knows Jobs are worth some money.

Jobs in San Francisco seem to be considerably more attractive than those found in Philadelphia, Billings, or Oklahoma City. In West Virginia Jobs are found underground. Jobs are hardly found at all in Detroit. Although Jobs may be everywhere, if you lose one it is difficult to find another.

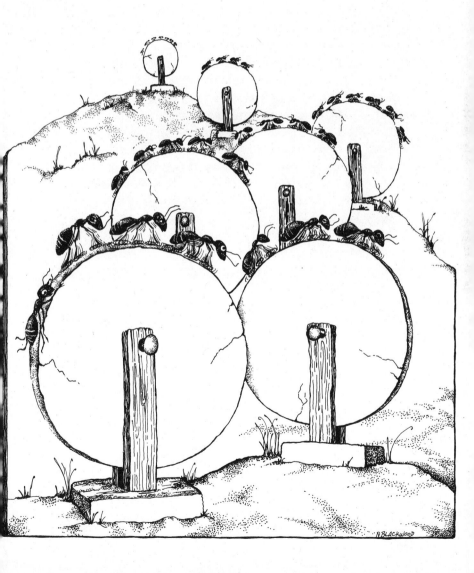

THE STRIKE

Birth of this nocturnal beast usually occurs at midnight, Saturday. The gestation period is a difficult time, fraught with the unexpected. Strikes live in groups called unions. The group is dominated by the union boss whose authority is rarely challenged. Strikes may unexpectedly appear from the remotest part of the jungle. There is an unsettling feeling when one is near, and a great deal of squawking occurs whenever Strikes appear. Before it appears, the Strike always attempts to demonstrate its power and virility. It bellows unreasonable demands. It boasts of unemployment insurance and union payments. It drags red herrings across its trail to confuse adversaries. The temperament of this beast may be downright mean, sometimes savage. With their neurotic displays of self-destruction, Strikes have few admirers. Nevertheless, Strikes associate with Shutdowns and Walkouts, creatures usually less fierce.

The Strike's life ends only when an acceptable offer is right on target. This weapon is usually manufactured through negotiation and compromise.

THE AGGRESSIVE SALES FORCE

This nomadic creature is always on the road yet it keeps within its own territory, an area that is jealously protected. It lives in a Holiday Inn. When young it lives in a school. But it is born, not to spell, but to sell. So the Sales Force travels the beaten path.

You always know when this sociable beast is around. Its stories are unmistakable. It eats what the Client eats. It is always reaching for tabs. On the outside it is always laughing, telling you how much it is worth. Inside, it worries about quotas, commissions, and alcoholism.

It likes its foot in the door. Once inside, it is always closing.

Taken out of the territory and put in organizational captivity most are not productive. Many perish. They yearn for the freedom of the wild, the traveling life, and, most of all, the Expense Account.

THE U.S. ECONOMY

The U.S. Economy is a monolithic beast said to be losing its competitiveness. Harder working, more industrious Economies in Japan and West Germany are growing, making much larger gains than this aging mammothlike creature.

Some predict that the growth of the U.S. Economy has ended and many wonder what to do with a No-Growth Economy. Social security does not seem to be the answer.

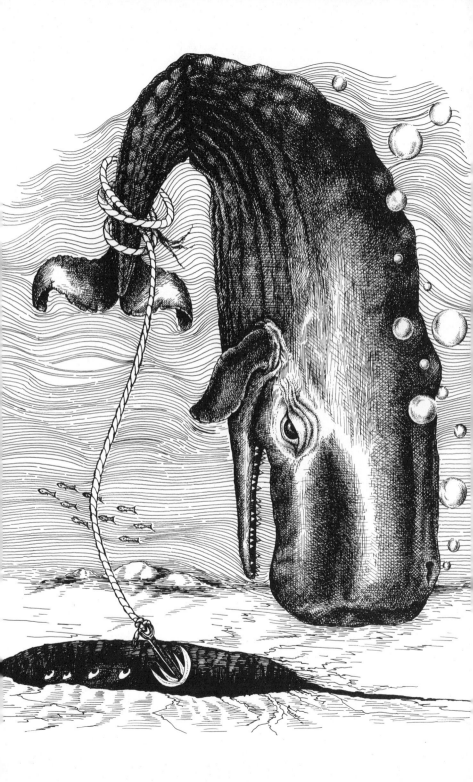

THE ECONOMISTS

Economists come in two sizes: Micro and Macro. The radical difference between these two pundits is surprising since they both feed upon assumptions.

There is an old legend about the Economists worth telling. A shipwrecked trio consisting of a Chemist, a Physicist, and an Economists was washed up on a small island. After a few days without food, a wooden crate containing canned goods fortunately washed ashore. Immediately, all agreed the problem was one of opening the cans of food. The Chemist proudly suggested that salt water placed on the tops of the cans would rust them open in a few weeks. The Physicist argued that this method, although scientifically valid, would take far too long. An alternative, utilizing the principles of physics, would be to carry a large rock and climb to the top of a tree. Then, projecting the rock downward at such an angle that the can would split open upon impact. The Economists, who had listened carefully to his colleagues, suggested they were both wrong. The solution was similar to other economic solutions. He proudly announced "We just assume we have a can opener."

Don't bet the rent money if someone says this is an apocryphal story. In addition to feeding on every possible type of assumption, the Macro Economists makes a lot of noise about the future, how to improve output, and how to encourage investment. However, the sounds you hear change every six months. White House Economists tell you everything around the corner will be rosy if you just stay the course. They don't tell you about the jagged rocks on the course between tight monetary policy and loose fiscal policy.

The Micro Economists is quite marginal.

THE CASH COW

The Cash Cow is milked for all its worth. You'd think an old friend would get better treatment than this. But, because it gives money, not milk, the cash flow is all that counts. Its managers don't see much of a future for this aging beast, deprived of investment nourishment. They don't spend any money priming the pump; this cow is expected to give but not take. This Cow is milked and milked until the cash flow becomes a cash trickle.

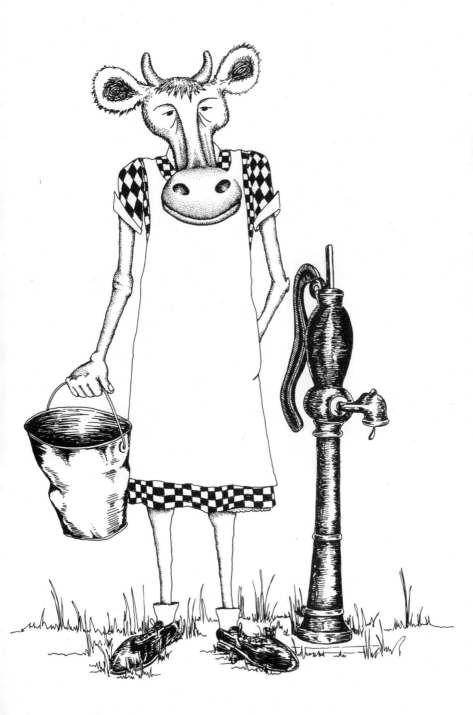

THE THIRTY-SECOND COMMERCIAL

True, there always has been a degree of contempt associated with the Commercial; this breed has been accused of deception and dishonesty. Some are extremely irritating. Commercials make you want to take an aspirin because of your headache, or worry about your aching backache.

Commercials aren't made the way they used to be. There was a time when most of these creatures were twice as long. But, with nothing permanent except change, this beast finds its extremely short life span getting shorter. Does it matter? After all, one only needs a slice-of-life for a place in the sun. However, this cannot be why many Commercials are called spot.

Some Commercials are pleasingly musical. Some sing. Others dance. The Coca-Cola Commercial tried to teach the world to sing in perfect harmony. After listening to a Jingle Commercial like this, you may hum its song over and over again until you are maddened by it. Commercials may be very emotional. AT&T Commercials make you want to reach out and touch someone. Marlboro Commercials make you feel very masculine.

Purchasing a Commercial may be expensive. A Super Bowl Commercial may cost more than $500,000.

THE CAREFREE VACATION

The Carefree Vacation may be seen soaring, like Jonathan Livingston Seagull, above factories and offices on its way to greener grasses and whiter sands. Worryfree, save whether the sun will shine, the Vacation's main purpose in life is to have fun. And it does.

Vacations are also known as the Annual Leave, the Furlough, and "the best thing about this darn job."

Flocks of Vacationers are a familiar sight to resort dwellers. Vacationers seem to be continually hungry, constantly looking out for their next meal. They congregate around hamburger stands, snack bars, and all-you-can-eat restaurants. They are found just about anywhere there is something to eat.

Vacations are found flying and smiling everywhere. However a Vacation in Tahiti, Europe, or Acapulco is more glamorous. Vacations with the least glamour fly directly toward relatives and stay for two weeks. A Vacation that flies toward Toledo rather than Aspen maybe flying for obligation rather than relaxation.

THE GOLDEN OPPORTUNITY

This fantastic creature leads the way to the good life. Seize the Golden Opportunity whenever you see it. According to corporate legend, the Golden Opportunity will enter the office building, ride the elevator up to your floor, and knock at your door. Of course, playful Opportunities will dress themselves up as something else so that you don't recognize them. You must realize the Golden Opportunity uses sleight-of-hand tricks. Knowing if you have encountered a true Golden Opportunity rather than a mere Alternative is, however, the real trick. Pay attention to the Opportunity's essence, not its trappings.

Be sure to take along a pair of riding boots and some insight. Remember, a lot of damn fool things have been said about Golden Opportunities.

FINIS